Reproducible

JELLY-BEAN EASTER

Three Dramas for Children

Abingdon Press
Nashville

A JELLYBEAN EASTER

ISBN 0-687-07615-3

03 04 05 06 07 08 09 10 11 12 - 10 9 8 7 6 5 4 3 2 1

Manufactured in the United States of America

CONTENTS

A Jellybean Easter

by Shirley Lockhart Ingram

Production Notes

The Easter story is simply told through the inquisitiveness of children as they acquire an understanding at their own age level. The play would be appropriate during the Easter Sunday morning worship service. Playing time is about twenty-five minutes. Only one or two rehearsals are needed.

Props

Clear glass container, package of jellybeans, palm branches (can be made from construction paper or crepe paper.)

Older Child: What is Easter? Is it a time to rejoice or to cry? A time to celebrate or to be sad? What is Easter?

Child 1: Easter is a special day in the life of the church.

Child 2: Last Sunday was Palm Sunday. The people waved palm branches. (*The other children wave palm branches.*) The people gathered to see Jesus.

Child 1: Why did they wave palm branches?

Child 2: When Jesus rode into Jerusalem on a donkey, the people lined the sides of the road. Some spread their garments on the road. Others cut the palm branches down to make a carpet for this man called Jesus. They waved their palm branches and shouted:

All Children: Hosanna! Hosanna! Blessed is he who comes in the name of the Lord.

Child 3: Today is Easter Sunday! It is an exciting day because we celebrate the day Jesus rose from the dead. God gave Jesus his life back again on Easter.

All the children sing "This Is the Day" or a hymn of your choice. If you have two groups of children, the second group can echo the song for the second verse.

Older Child: Easter reminds us of many things. Can you name some?

Each child drops a specific colored jellybean into a glass container that is visible to the audience as he or she speaks:

Child 1: Red is for the blood he gave.

Child 2: Green is for the grass that was created.

Child 3: Yellow is for the sun so bright.

Child 4: Orange is for the sunset at night.

Child 5: Black is for the sins humankind has made.

Child 6: White is for his pure life.

Child 7: Purple is for his hour of sorrow.

Child 8: Pink is for our new tomorrow.

Older Child: Thank you, children. A jar of jellybeans, colorful and sweet, is a prayer, is a promise, is a special treat. Easter is a time to celebrate a new life for all of us. What can we celebrate?

Child 1: Green grass.

Child 2: Beautiful flowers.

Child 3: Colorful butterflies.

Child 4: Sunny days.

Child 5: Our families.

Child 6: Our friends.

Child 7: Our church.

Child 8: Sleep and rest.

Child 9: And the life of Jesus.

OLDER CHILD *or Pastor reads John 3:16.*

All Children: Hallelujah! Hallelujah! Happy, happy Easter!

Pastor or Teacher announces a congregational hymn. Suggestions include "Alleluia," "Morning Has Broken," "This Is My Father's World," "He Lives," or "Christ the Lord Is Risen Today."

Pastor or Teacher closes with a benediction.

THE EASTER STORY

by Shirley Lockhart Ingram

Production Notes

The familiar Easter story begins with the children celebrating Palm Sunday. The events of Holy Week are told in Scripture, pantomime, and hymns. Lighting is important in scenery changes. For use in a small church, different roles can be interchangeable, such as the children's choir. All hymns are one verse, except the congregational hymn, "Christ the Lord Is Risen Today." These hymns are found in The United Methodist Hymnal. *Most costumes can be simple robes such as those worn in Bible times.*

Props

Big jar or jug, chairs and long table for the Last Supper scene, three rugged crosses, a big rock (can be made from a large cardboard box painted gray) for the garden of Gethsemane scene, palm branches, drums or cymbals.

Cast

Bible Reader
Seven Children (who can also play the disciples' roles)
Woman With a Jar
Man Carrying a Jar
Two Females
Youth and/or Adult Choir
Man Receiving Silver From Judas
Angel

Playing Time: 45 minutes

Scene 1

Children enter from back of sanctuary waving palm branches and shouting: "Hosanna! Hosanna! Blessed is he who comes in the name of the Lord. Hosanna in the highest! Blessed is he who comes in the name of the Lord." They stand to one side of the chancel area.

Reader: Matthew 21:1-11.

CHILD 1: (*Steps forward*) Glory in the highest!

CHILD 2: (*Stands to opposite side of* CHILD 1) Why are you shouting? What is going on?

CHILD 1: Make way for Jesus of Nazareth.

CHILD 2: Who is he?

CHILD 3: (*Steps forward*) He is the prophet from Galilee.

CHILD 2: What's so special about him?

CHILD 3: He heals the sick.

CHILD 4: He feeds the poor.

CHILD 5: He casts out demons.

CHILD 6: He forgives our sins.

CHILD 2: No man on earth can do all this. Get real!

CHILD 7: He is the Son of God . . . Lord of Lords, King of Kings!

ALL: (*except* CHILD 2) Hosanna . . . Hosanna. Blessed is he who comes in the name of the Lord!

(*Lights dim*)

Scene 2
(*Crowd dressed in robes gathers in a huddle.*)
Reader: Matthew 21:12-22.
(*The children sing "Tell Me the Stories of Jesus."*)

Scene 3
(*Peter, James, and John sit in a semicircle with a gap signifying Jesus. They are chattering among themselves.*)
Reader: Mark 13:3-8.
(*The children sing, "Do, Lord, Remember Me."*)

Scene 4
(*Peter, James, and John watch as a woman mimes pouring oil over an empty chair signifying Jesus. They mumble.*)
Reader: Mark 14:1-9.
(*The teen or adult choir sings, "We've a Story to Tell to the Nations."*)

Scene 5
(*Judas receives thirty pieces of silver from someone.*)
Reader: Mark 14:10-11.
(*The children sing, "It's Me, It's Me, O Lord."*)

Scene 6
(*Last Supper scene; the disciples sit around a table with an empty chair in the middle. Two disciples talk to a man carrying a jar and follow him to right of stage.*)
Reader: Mark 14:12-25.
(*Each* DISCIPLE *asks: "Is it I?" Both choirs sing, "Let Us Break Bread Together."*)

Scene 7
(*Garden scene; Peter, James, and John act drowsy and then go to sleep.*)
Reader: Mark 14:26-42.
(*Both choirs sing, "Sweet Hour of Prayer."*)

Scene 8
(*Three crosses are dragged in and held upright.*)
Reader: Mark 15:16.

Both Choirs: Hail, King of the Jews . . . Aha! You who would destroy the Temple and build it in three days, save yourself or come down from the cross. He saved others . . . he cannot save himself. Let the Christ, the King of Israel (*Laugh*) come down from the cross that we may see and believe.

(*The adult choir sings "Alas! and Did My Savior Bleed."*)

Scene 9
(*Lights go out and a loud noise from drums or cymbals plays.*)
Reader: Mark 15:33-39.
(*The adult choir sings: "Were You There" The adult choir hums the second verse and sings the chorus again.*)

Scene 10
(*Garden scene; two women enter and look at the big rock. They see the angel sitting outside. They run away and meet the other disciples and tell them. They chatter.*)
Reader: Mark 16:1-8.

(*Invite the congregation to stand and sing, "Christ the Lord Is Risen Today."*)

(*Close with a benediction.*)

Son Power Saves the Day

by Shelba Nivens and Dawn Nivens

Use as a short play or as five scenes,
one each day for Vacation Bible School or Sunday school.

Synopsis

Jan and Matthew set out for Camp Serve-a-Lot to serve Jesus. With them is the "Son Power Pack"—Laughter, Love, Praise, and Prayer. Along the road toward camp, they encounter enemies—Quarreling, Anger, Gloom, Prejudice, and Discouragement. The Son Power Pack—Prayer, Laughter, Love, and Praise—helps them fight off these enemies and get to their destination, which turns out to be an unexpected and surprising place.

Props

Rocks, either real or constructed (see Production Notes), including two rocks large enough to sit on and hide behind
Trees
Bushes
Plants
Vines
Concealed ladder or other high spot
Road marker sign reading "Camp Serve-a-Lot Just Ahead"
Large banner reading "Welcome to Camp Serve-a-Lot"
Large poster showing a world map and reading "Your World"
See the list of characters for props carried by each person.

Production Notes

Drama might be used in a camp or a church setting. A rock for Matthew to sit on is downstage left. A rock at stage right conceals **DISCOURAGEMENT** until he jumps up. **GLOOM** might be lying on the floor concealed by his dark cape and bushes until time for him or her to appear as though coming up out of a hole in the ground. **PREJUDICE** should drop from a concealed ladder or other high spot as though jumping from a tree or a cliff. **QUARRELING** and **ANGER** are hidden behind trees or rocks. Scenery might be real rocks and trees if out-of-doors setting is used. Inside, use tree branches, plants, stools, benches, tables, boxes, sheeting, cardboard—whatever is handy—along with paint, to create scenery.

The trail to camp should lead around and over some of these trees and rocks to make the trip appear longer. It should lead across the stage from left to right, then curve back right again to center stage where Camp Serve-a-Lot is located. Conceal the "Camp Serve-a-Lot Just Ahead" sign behind vines.

Characters

Jan—wears camp clothes; carries a Bible and a bag with soap, a toothbrush, and so forth.
Matt—wears camp clothes; carries a Bible and a bag with soap, a toothbrush, and so forth.
Adult Leader (optional)—to encourage children's response to actors.
Stage Crew—at least four people to carry banner and poster.

Son Power Pack:
Prayer—a robust boy. Wears long, white cape (might use sheet) over Superman-type outfit underneath with large *P* on front. Walks with hands folded in prayer; may drop to knees when group stops. When he encounters enemy, jumps to feet with Superman stance and throws back cape to reveal costume underneath.

Love—a pleasant-faced girl. Wears long, soft-colored dress or robe. Might wear flowers in her hair. She is always hugging everyone.

Laughter—a bright, happy girl or boy. Wears clothes with a lot of happy colors in them, maybe a colorful crazy-looking outfit. He or she has a big happy laugh and laughs a lot (softly, as if someone else is talking that only he or she can hear).

Praise—a happy, joyful boy or girl who can sing. Wears bright pleasant-looking clothes, maybe a sunny-looking outfit (not wild-looking clothes like Laughter wears). He or she claps hands praising God and might lift hands in praise as he or she moves along.

Enemies:

Quarreling—girl or boy made up to look ugly, scary, or evil, with claws, mask, long tail, and evil-looking weapon. May be bloody-looking or wear bandages.

Anger—girl or boy made up to look ugly, scary, or evil, with claws, mask, long tail, and evil-looking weapon. May be bloody-looking or wear bandages.

Gloom—in black mask and black hooded robe from head to toe. Has long rope made of breakable strips or twisted paper to "bind" people.

Prejudice—ugly with claws and droopy wings. Jumps from table, ladder, or something high. Or may be a dummy that's dropped from elevated spot as children walk by.

Discouragement—girl or boy fully covered in hooded, dull-covered cloak.

(*As scene opens,* MATT *sits on rock downstage left with back to audience—in front of curtains, if curtains are used.*)

(JAN *enters up aisle, singing and skipping. She is singing "Jesus Wants Me for a Sunbeam" or another happy song of your choosing. This song will be repeated throughout the drama.*)

MATT: (*Turns to face* JAN) Hi, Jan. Where are you going?

JAN: Hi, Matt. I'm going to Camp Serve-a-Lot.

MATT: Camp Serve-a-Lot? What are you going to do there?

JAN: See friends, laugh, play, have a good time. And we help people and tell them about Jesus. It's a place where everyone serves Jesus.

MATT: Sounds great! Can I come too?

JAN: Do you want to serve Jesus?

MATT: Of course. All Christian boys and girls want to serve Jesus. But I don't know if I can.

JAN: Sure you can. You have the power.

MATT: Power? What power?

JAN: When you asked Jesus to come into your heart, he gave you power to serve him. Now you have the Son Power Pack you can call on for help.

MATT: (*Loudly, in surprise*) Son Power Pack?!?

(LAUGHTER, LOVE, PRAISE, *and* PRAYER *rush onstage.*)

LAUGHTER: Did someone call us?

MATT: (*Jumps back in surprise*) Who are you?

(LAUGHTER, LOVE, PRAISE, *and* PRAYER *line up like cheerleaders giving cheer. They sing out loudly, emphasizing their words with hand actions.*)

POWER PACK: We're the S-O-N, Son Power Pack!

PRAYER: (*Steps forward, hands folded in prayer*) I'm Prayer.

PRAISE: (*Steps forward, lifts hands in praise*) I'm Praise.

LOVE: (*Hugs Matt*) I'm Love.

MATT: (*Pulls away and looks at* JAN) Does she have to do that?

LAUGHTER: (*Steps forward, laughing aloud*) I'm Laughter.

JAN: See, Matt, they're the power to help us serve Jesus. So, come on, gang. (*Motions everyone forward*) Let's go. Coming, Matt?

MATT: Sure. I'm right with you.

JAN: (*To audience*) Would you like to come with us? Do you want to learn to serve Jesus? (*Pause for response*) Great! You can stay right where you are and still come with us by just loosening your imagination and letting it come along. How about it? Do you have a good imagination? (*Pause for response*) Then let it loose! And here we go!

(*Curtains open or lights come up onstage.*)

(JAN, MATT, LAUGHTER, LOVE, *and* PRAISE *move onstage right, singing "Jesus Wants Me for a Sunbeam" or the song sung earlier by* JAN.)

PRAYER: (*Calls out from offstage*) Hey! You're forgetting something!

(JAN *and* MATT *look around in surprise.*)

JAN AND MATT: (*Look quizzically at each other.*) We are?

MATT: (*Lifts Bible*) I have my Bible.

JAN: I have mine too. (*To audience*) Do you have yours? (*Pause for response*) Well, let's see what else we have. (*Pulls items from bag, encouraging audience to call out name of items with her*) Here's my toothbrush . . . hair brush . . . swimsuit . . . towel . . . I seem to have everything. What could we be forgetting? (*Pause for audience response.*)

PRAYER: (*Dancing up and down, waving arms for attention*) Me! It's me! You're forgetting me!

JAN: Prayer! Yes, we are forgetting Prayer. We always need prayer when we start out on a trip. Come on, let's go back for Prayer.

(*Everyone walks back to* PRAYER, *forms prayer circle.* JAN *asks audience to bow heads with them, then prays, asking Jesus to protect them and guide them as they seek to serve God, and to help them overcome temptation to do wrong.*)

JAN: Now we're ready to travel! Come on, everyone. (*Motions forward*) Let's go! Sing!

(THE SON POWER PACK *blends in with the background scenery as much as possible until needed. The audience is encouraged to sing along with* JAN *and* MATT *as they move stage right along the trail toward Camp. Use the song sung earlier.* QUARRELING *and* ANGER *slip up behind and whisper in the ears of* JAN *and* MATT.)

JAN: (*Turns to* MATT *angrily, yells*) Matt! Why didn't you let me borrow a pencil yesterday at school when I asked?

MATT: (*Angrily*) I told you I had only one, and I needed it!

(QUARRELING *and* ANGER *nod and laugh silently, encouraging them to quarrel. They snarl and shake them, and make motions like they want to fist fight.*)

JAN: Yeah? Well, I needed it too.

MATT: But it was mine.

JAN: (*Shakes* MATT *angrily*) But I wanted it! You were being stingy. (*Stops shaking* MATT) What am I saying? Why am I doing this? I'm not serving Jesus when I behave this way.

(ANGER *whispers in her ear and puts her hand on* MATT*'s shoulder.*)

JAN: (*Shakes* MATT) Yeah, that's right. You're stingy.

MATT: Yeah? Well, you're selfish. (*Stops*) Why am I saying this? I don't mean it.

(QUARRELING *whispers in his ear.*)

MATT: (*Angrily to* JAN) You always get angry when you don't get your way.

JAN: No, I don't. You know I don't.

MATT: Yeah? You're angry now, aren't you?

JAN: But it's all your fault.

MATT: No, it's not. You're the one who— (*Stops, looks around and sees their enemy, tries to push them off*) Look! It's Quarreling and Anger. They are making us angry and quarrelsome.

JAN: Quick! We need some help here! (*To audience*) Who can we call to help us? (*Pause for response.*)

MATT: Yes! Call Love. Love can help us beat Quarreling and Anger. Help me, everyone. Help me call Love. (*Motions for audience to join in calling.*)

EVERYONE: (*Calls*) Love! Love, where are you? Help! We need help.

LOVE: (*Rushes up, starts hugging* JAN *and* MATT) I'm here! I'm here! All you have to do is call.

JAN: Matt, I'm sorry I called you stingy. I'm the one who was acting ugly.

MATT: I'm sorry, too, Jan, for calling you names. And I'm sorry I didn't let you borrow my pencil. I could have shared it. (*Extends hand*) Friends again? Shake?

(JAN *and* MATT *shake hands.* LOVE *puts arms around them both in a big hug.*)

QUARRELING: Ugh! Yuck! All that mush! I can't bear to look. (*Hides face against his arm and turns away.*)

ANGER: And I can't bear to listen. (*Puts fingers in ears and turns away.*)

(JAN, MATT, *and* LOVE *stop hugging, look at enemies, look at each other—and audience, nod and smile. All three run over to hug* QUARRELING *and* ANGER. QUARRELING *and* ANGER *struggle to get loose.*)

ANGER: (*Stops struggling*) Hey, Quarreling! This is sort of nice—being loved.

QUARRELING: It is? (*Stops struggling and lets them hug him.*) Yeah, I didn't know. Love was so nice. Nobody ever loved me before.

ANGER: Ahhh. It's like a warm, fuzzy blanket. I could get used to this.

QUARRELING: You know, I think I'll change my name.

EVERYONE: (*Stops hugging and steps back to look at* QUARRELING.) You will? What will you change it to?

QUARRELING: Let's see. (*Puts chin in hand thoughtfully.*) I think I might like to be called Peace from now on.

JAN, MATT, LOVE: Peace? That's great, Quarreling. (*Look at one another and laugh.*)

JAN: We mean—that's great, Peace. Peace is a great name. (*Looks at audience, nodding for them to agree.*)

ANGER: Yeah, I kind of like that. What can I change my name to?

JAN: What do you think, kids? What would be a good new name for Anger, now that he's not angry anymore? (*Pauses for response.*)

JAN, MATT, LOVE: (*Chin in hand, thinking*) Umm. Umm, let's see.

MATT: (*Brightly*) Forgiveness! That's it. Anger could be replaced with Forgiveness. What do you think? (*Pauses for audience response, then to* ANGER) How about it? Why don't you be Forgiveness now?

ANGER: (*Thoughtfully*) Forgiveness. Umm. Forgiveness. Yeah, that has a nice ring to it. I'll be Forgiveness.

JAN: OK. And now that we have that settled, we'd better be going.

FORGIVENESS: Will you stop by to see us again sometime?

PEACE: We live just over the hill there. (*Points left.*)

JAN, MATT: Sure, we would like that.

JAN: (*Hands Bible to them*) Here, read this. It's a Bible and tells about Jesus. We'll stop by on our way back and talk to you about what you've read.

FORGIVENESS, PEACE: OK. We'll read it. See you later.

(LOVE, JAN, *and* MATT *hug them. They hug back, say goodbyes, wave.* FORGIVENESS *and* PEACE *exit left as* LOVE *slips along behind them.*)

JAN: (*To audience*) Isn't this a great trip? Come on and sing with us.

(*They begin singing the happy song sung earlier as* JAN *and* MATT *continue on trip.* GLOOM *slips along behind rocks or trees, keeping up with them. He carries or drags rope, watching for an opportunity to attack. Audience can see him, but* JAN *and* MATT *cannot.*)

MATT: (*Stops singing, looks toward spot where* GLOOM *is hidden. Grabs* JAN*'s arm*) Jan! Look!

(JAN *stops singing, turns to look.*)

MATT: Did you see something black move over there? (*Points*)

JAN: No. All I see are trees and bushes and flowers.

(*They begin singing again.* GLOOM *darts to a hiding place close to them. Lights dim.*)

MATT: (*Stops singing and looks around*) Jan?

(JAN *keeps singing and walking.*)

MATT: (*Louder*) Jan! (*Grabs her arm and shakes*) Jan! Stop!

(JAN *stops singing and walking.*)

MATT: Have you noticed how dark and gloomy it's getting?

JAN: No. Not until you mentioned it. I suddenly don't feel so well, though. I feel all—all down and out and—sort of—gloomy.

MATT: Me too.

(*They look around as though frightened. Suddenly, from behind them,* GLOOM *pounces, growling and hissing, and wraps rope around them. They drop their bags, spilling the contents.*)

GLOOM: I've got you now, you happy, singing, silly children. You won't be joyful anymore. (*Wraps rope around and around them.*)

(*Lights grow dimmer.*)

JAN, MATT: (*Moaning, whining*) I feel so sad. I'm so unhappy. Everything looks so dark.

(*They sink to ground and sit silently as* GLOOM *moves around and around them, sprinkling dark powder on them while chanting.*)

Gloom: I'm gloom and doom.
I put you down.
I make you unhappy.
You wear a frown.

You sigh and cry.
Can't get away.
I wrap you in gloom.
You're my slave.

Jan: Oh, no, Matt! We've been captured by dark, ugly Gloom. What will we do?

Matt: Maybe we can call on the Power Pack.

Jan: I don't know. It's so dark and gloomy, they may not be able to find us.

Gloom: (*Chanting*) I'm gloom and doom, I get you down . . .

(LAUGHTER *begins laughing. Lights grow brighter.*)

Gloom: (*Stops chanting, looks around*) Oh, no! It's Laughter. Everything is getting brighter.

(*Laughter gets louder.*)

Jan: Listen! It is Laughter. She found us. Things are getting bright again. Hurry! Sit up straight. Laugh. Chase away that old, dark Gloom.

(JAN *and* MATT *sit up straight, start laughing loudly.*)

Gloom: (*Covers ears*) No, no! Stop! Stop that silly laughter. Don't you know Laughter chases away gloom?

Jan: (*Happily*) Yes, we know. (*To audience*) Come on, kids, help us. Be joyful. Laugh!

(*Everyone laughs loudly as* LAUGHTER *helps* JAN *and* MATT *stand and break the ropes from around them.*)

Gloom: Nooo! No! No! No! No! (*Backs away with hands up in front of her face.*)

(JAN *moves slowly forward toward* GLOOM *in long steps, begins singing and motioning for everyone to sing with her.* JAN *sings "The Joy of the Lord Is My Strength" or a song of your choice.*)

Gloom: (*Hands over ears, twisting and turning in anguish*) Stop! Stop! I can't bear it! (*Turns and runs.*)

(JAN, MATT, *and* LAUGHTER *chase her offstage left, laughing.* JAN *and* MATT *return, still laughing, pick up bags and contents, continue on their trip, singing "The Joy of the Lord" or the song you chose.*)

(PREJUDICE *suddenly swoops down on* JAN. *If a person, he hangs around her neck from behind. If a dummy, it might be dropped or pitched on her, but be sure it's big and floppy and lightweight.*)

Jan: (*Screams, reaches up, and feels* PREJUDICE *holding onto her.*) Something grabbed me, Matt! It's holding onto me!

Matt: I'll get if off. (*Moves to help her.*)

Jan: No! Don't touch me! I don't want you near me.

Matt: What do you mean? I'm your friend.

JAN: My friend! Ha! You're no friend of mine. I don't want to be seen with you. My family has more money than your family. I dress better than you do. And you look different! Your skin is not the same color as mine.

MATT: Why, Jan, I didn't know you were prejudiced.

JAN: Prejudiced? Of course I'm NOT prejudiced.

MATT: Did you hear all the things you just said? It sounded to me like you were being prejudiced.

JAN: Yeah, it did. I wonder . . . Hey! Stop pulling my hair! (*Slaps at* PREJUDICE) What does this thing look like? (*To audience*) Quick! Describe it to me. What does it look like?

(MATT *encourages audience to help him as he begins describing* PREJUDICE.)

JAN: (*Knocking at* PREJUDICE) Get him off me! Quick, Matt! Get him off! It's that old ugly sin Prejudice. That's why I said those awful things to you.

(MATT *begins trying to pull him off, but can't.*)

JAN: Matt, I'm starting to hate you again. Hurry, call on Love to help us! And Prayer too! (*To audience*) Come on, kids, help us. Call Love and Prayer.

(*As everyone calls for* LOVE *and* PRAYER *to help,* MATT *keeps pulling at* PREJUDICE, *but can't get him loose.*)

LOVE, PRAYER: (*Rush up*) We're here. We're here. We can give you power to overcome Prejudice.

(PRAYER *kneels, folds hands in prayer.* LOVE *hugs* JAN *and* PREJUDICE.)

PREJUDICE: (*Turns loose, pulls away, and starts to run off*) Let me get out of here!

LOVE: Wait, don't run. We just want to love you.

PREJUDICE: No! You're not good enough to love me. I'm better than you. (*Runs left.*)

JAN, MATT, LOVE: But we want to help you. (*Watch sadly as* PREJUDICE *exits.*)

JAN: That's so sad. Prejudice just doesn't know how to love.

LOVE: I'll go after him and try again to win him. Love never gives up.

PRAYER: I'll go too. Prayer changes things.

(LOVE *and* PRAYER *exit.*)

JAN: Matt, I'm sorry I said those ugly things to you. Will you forgive me?

MATT: Yes, of course I forgive you. I'm happy you had the power to defeat Prejudice. Oh, look! There's a sign. Let's see what it says. Help me uncover it, Jan. (*They remove vines and so forth.*)

JAN: What does it say? (*To audience*) Can you read it? Ummm— (*Encouraging audience to read with her*) It says Camp Serve-a-Lot just ahead. Great! We're almost there. Let's go. (*Motions onward*)

DISCOURAGEMENT: (*Suddenly pops up to block the way*) Oh, no you don't! You can't make it any further. You know you're too tired to go on.

MATT: (*Drags to a stop, groaning, sighing*) I am suddenly soooo tired.

JAN: No! Don't let him stop you. It's wicked Discouragement! We must go on. We're almost there.

MATT: But I'm too tired. (*Sits down or sprawls on ground*) We've walked a long way. We've been through a lot of stuff. We've had to fight off a lot of enemies.

JAN: Yes, we have. But don't forget we have power. (*Runs to help Matt.*)

DISCOURAGEMENT: Power! Ha! What power? All your power has gone. Look around you. Do you see any power?

JAN: (*Looks around. The* SON POWER PACK *is out of sight.*) No, I don't. Maybe we don't have power anymore, Matt. I'm awfully tired too. And hungry. I don't think I can go on, either. What can we do?

(PRAISE *begins singing a praise song offstage.*)

JAN: It's Praise. She's singing praises. Stand up. Sing with her. Praise can chase away discouragement.

DISCOURAGEMENT: No, it can't. I'm too strong! And you're too weak. You won't be able to climb the hill to the camp gate. It's too steep and you're too tired. The road is rocky.

JAN: We can make it. I know we can. Stand up. Sing. (*To audience*) Come on, everyone, help us. Sing with us. (*Begins singing the praise song.*)

(MATT *stands up, begins singing. They take high labored steps as though trying to climb a steep hill. They stop to yell out in pain and rub feet, then go on singing and trudging up hill.* PRAISE *joins them, singing.* STAGE CREW *raises "Welcome to Camp Serve-a-Lot" banner upstage center.*)

JAN: Look, everyone! There it is—Camp Serve-a-Lot! We're almost there. We're going to make it.

(DISCOURAGEMENT *tries to block the way, pushes them down. They get up, keep singing and moving.* DISCOURAGEMENT *puts rocks, limbs in their way. They go around or over and keep moving and singing.* PRAYER, LOVE, *and* LAUGHTER *follow them, singing.*)

JAN: (*Looks back*) It's the rest of the Power Pack. We have all the power we need to make it. Come on, kids, keep singing.

(*Everyone steps over and around obstacles, pushes* DISCOURAGEMENT *aside, sings and climbs.* DISCOURAGEMENT *lets out a loud yell, puts arms over his head and runs offstage right.*)

JAN, MATT: (*Stop and watch him go*) Look! Look! We've chased Discouragement away. There he goes! Yea! (*Encourages audience to cheer*)

JAN: (*Lifts hand to silence audience*) Thank you, everyone. You can sit down now. (*Waits for quiet*) You've done a great job, helping us chase away the enemy. And look! We've reached Camp Serve-a-Lot! (*Indicates banner*)

MATT: (*Moves upstage center, looks around, confused, turns all the way around looking*) Where? Where is Camp Serve-a-Lot, Jan? I see the sign, but I don't see a camp. (*Scratches head, staring stage left.*)

(STAGE HANDS *enter right with "Your World" poster.*)

MATT: (*With back to poster, looks around stage for camp*) Where is Camp Serve-a-Lot? (*To audience*) Do you see a camp? What am I missing here?

(JAN *stands behind* MATT, *indicates the poster to audience, silently expresses amusement at* MATT*'s confusion, mouths "right here," pointing to spot where she stands.* MATT *continues to search in confusion.*)

JAN: (*Cups hands around mouth to call*) Look be-hinnnnd you.

MATT: (*Turns around a few times, stops to stare at banner and poster*) Camp Serve-a-Lot. That's what the sign says, but . . . (*Scratches head, puts finger to chin, thoughtfully*) Ummm . . . A map of the world . . . I wonder . . .

JAN: (*Points to slogan over the map, prompts audience to read with her*) Your world.

MATT: Oh, I get it! I CAN see Camp Serve-a-Lot. (*To audience*) Can you? Can you see it? Do you know where Camp Serve-a-Lot is? It's our world. Our whole world! Wherever we live, and play and go to school. This is Camp Serve-a-Lot. Right, Jan?

JAN: That's right, Matt. We can serve Jesus wherever we are. (*The Son Power Pack moves over to stand beside them.*) And we can have the Power Pack—Laughter, Love, Praise, and Prayer—to help us when Jesus—who gives us the power to serve him—is in our hearts.

(*An adult leader might share the way we let Jesus into our hearts, and pray with anyone who would like to invite him in. End with a song.*)